WOODWINDS

AN INTRODUCTION TO MUSICAL INSTRUMENTS

By Dee Lillegard

CHILDRENS PRESS ®

CHICAGO

PHOTO CREDITS
Journalism Services:

© H. Rick Bamman—16
© Paul F. Gero—9 (top), 13, 23 (left)
© Mike Kidulich—9 (bottom), 23 (right), 24
© John Patsch—11
© James F. Quinn—cover, 20, 25, 26, 27, 28

Nawrocki Stock Photo:

© Michael Brohm—7, 8, 19
© Jim Cudney—15
© Robert Lightfoot—4, 6, 12, 14, 17, 21, 22
© Ken Sexton—5
© J. Steere—backcover, 3, 29
© Carlos Vergara—18
© Jim Wright—10

Art on pages 30 and 31 by Tom Dunnington

Library of Congress Cataloging-in-Publication Data

Lillegard, Dee
  Woodwinds.

  Summary: A brief introduction to the musical
instruments of the woodwind family.
  1. Woodwind instruments—Juvenile literature.
[1. Woodwind instrument] I. Title.
ML3928.L54 1987   788'.05   87-18232
ISBN 0-516-02217-2

Toy saxophone

Blow across the top of a bottle. You can make a funny sound.

Blow a whistle. You can make a loud sound.

3

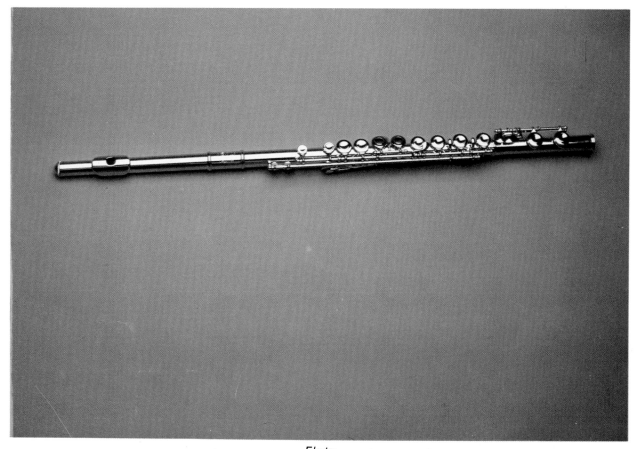

Flute

Here come the **woodwind** instruments! They make many sounds.

Hear that bright, clear sound? Is it a bird singing? No. It's a **flute**.

Woodwinds are played by blowing air into the instruments.

The **flute** can skip
quickly from note to note.
It can sound light and airy.
It can sound warm and soft,
too.

You hold the **flute** sideways and blow into a hole at one end. Keys cover other holes. Press the keys to play different notes.

Close-up of the keys on the flute

Flute player practices with the orchestra.

You can play the **flute** in
a symphony orchestra or in a
marching band. You can play
pop music or jazz, too.

Flutes are played in marching bands (above)
and in jazz bands (below).

Play the **piccolo**. The
piccolo is a baby flute. It
is shorter and its sounds are
higher.

Piccolos are played in Disneyland's
marching band.

The **piccolo** may be little,
but it makes a lot of noise.
It can make people laugh.

Flutes and oboes are woodwind instruments.

The **oboe** is different
from a flute. It uses reeds
to make sounds. Two small
pieces of cane or plastic fit
tightly into the hole at the

top. You blow air between the pieces of this *double-reed* to make sounds.

Oboes have double reeds.

Oboe section in symphony orchestra

It's hard to play the
oboe. You must hold it, press
the keys, and blow. You have
to keep stopping to breathe,
too!

Sometimes the **oboe** sounds sad. Sometimes it sounds weird—like something a snake charmer might play. It is often used for background music in television shows.

Snake charmer plays for a cobra.

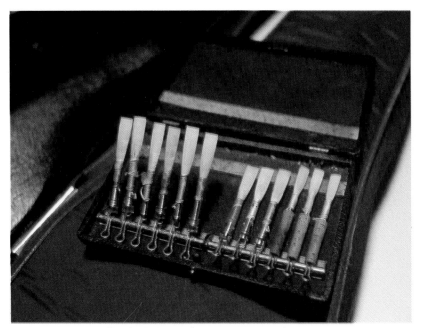

English horn (opposite page) uses double reeds (above).

The **English horn** is not English. It's not really a horn, either. It is a double-reed instrument with a bell shaped like an onion. It is longer than an oboe and sounds lower. Its tones can be rich or sad, and sometimes dreamy.

Bassoons have double reeds, too.

The **bassoon** looks like
two poles tied together with a
long, thin tongue sticking out.
It is a double-reed instrument.
Sometimes the **bassoon** is

called the "clown of the orchestra." It can make funny, low sounds. But it can make beautiful music, too.

It takes big hands to play the **bassoon**!

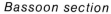

Bassoon section

Clarinets have a single reed.

Some woodwinds are *single-reed* instruments. They have only one reed attached to the mouthpiece.

The **clarinet** looks like the oboe. But it is a single-reed instrument.

Clarinets have a high clear sound.

You can play all sorts
of music on the **clarinet**. You
can make soft or loud sounds.
You can make mellow or
sharp sounds. You can play

22

very clear high notes.

You can play the **clarinet** in a symphony orchestra or in a small group. You can play it in a marching band or in a dance band.

A bass clarinet (right) has a different shape and sound than the regular clarinet (left).

Saxophones use a single reed.

Woodwinds are not always made of wood. They used to be. But today they are often made of metal.

The **saxophone** is made of brass. It is a single-reed instrument like the clarinet.

Soprano saxophones have a different shape than a tenor saxophone (opposite page).

Dance bands and jazz bands use sax players. The **saxophone** has a beautiful sound all its own.

Play a woodwind instrument
—a flute or an oboe, a big
bassoon, a clarinet, or a sax.
Play alone or with other
instruments.
Woodwinds can be fun!

*Baritone saxophones (opposite page) are
very big. They are woodwinds.*

♪ WIND INSTRUMENTS

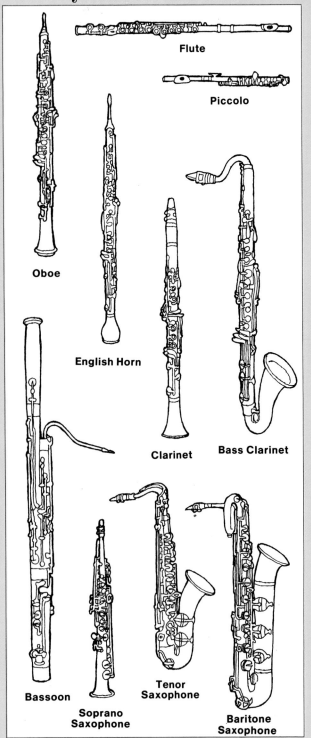

Flute

Piccolo

Oboe

English Horn

Clarinet

Bass Clarinet

Bassoon

Soprano Saxophone

Tenor Saxophone

Baritone Saxophone

♪ PERCUSSION INSTRUMENTS

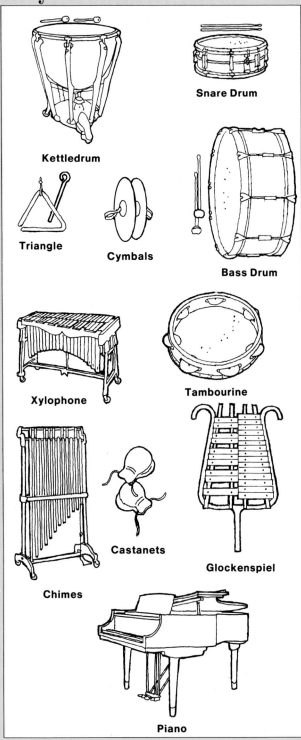

Kettledrum

Snare Drum

Triangle

Cymbals

Bass Drum

Xylophone

Tambourine

Chimes

Castanets

Glockenspiel

Piano

𝄞 STRINGED INSTRUMENTS

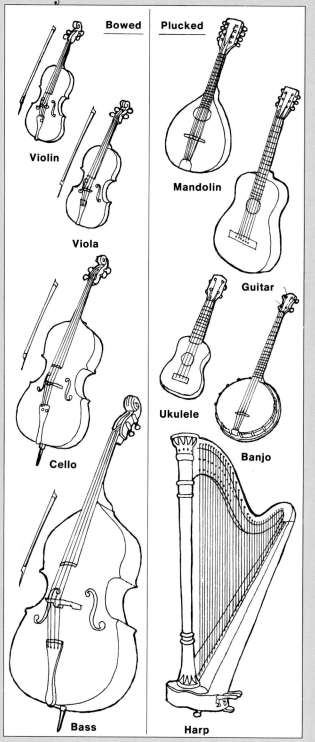

Bowed

Plucked

Violin

Viola

Mandolin

Guitar

Cello

Ukulele

Banjo

Bass

Harp

𝄞 BRASS INSTRUMENTS

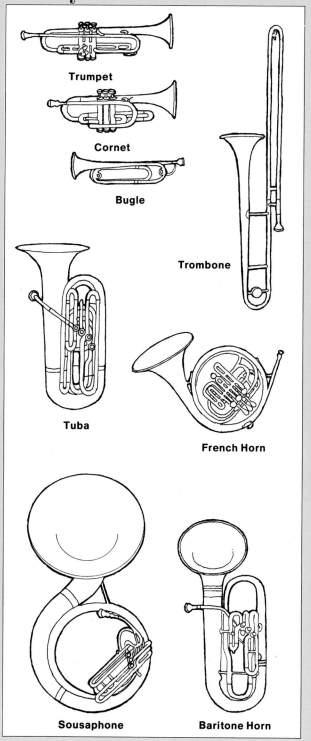

Trumpet

Cornet

Bugle

Trombone

Tuba

French Horn

Sousaphone

Baritone Horn

ABOUT THE AUTHOR

Dee Lillegard (born Deanna Quintel) is the author of over two hundred published stories, poems, and puzzles for children, plus *Word Skills*, a series of high-interest grammar worktests, and *September to September, Poems for All Year Round*, a teacher resource. Ms. Lillegard has also worked as a children's book editor and teaches writing for children in the San Francisco Bay Area. She is a native Californian.